THE INCREASING CASES OF WIFE BATTERING AND DOMESTIC VIOLENCE

A Deadly Syndrome In Our Society.

BY

Henry, Frederick

Copyright©2022

All rights reserved

TABLE OF CONTENTS

INTRODUCTION

Is There Any Justification For It?

As certain widespread misconceptions regarding battering revolve or are examined in the social and historical context, this article aims to address an assumption about battered women. It will offer some recommendations for both men's and women's responsibilities.

Wife abuse has existed for centuries, far longer than we can determine or prove. While some have adopted it, others have done away with it. We have all taken different actions to neither encourage nor stop it.

I took the time to carefully consider my remarks, gather my opinions, apply my knowledge to them, and then tie it all up in the context of my experiences and feelings as a victim of wife battering and domestic violence.

In recent years, wife or woman abuse has become more prevalent throughout our various societies and other areas.

The fact that nearly 50% of these battered women experienced their abuse in front of their kids still stands.

This book seeks to understand the underlying factors that contribute to a wife-beating as well as the psychological harm it causes to the victims and their children.

We have seen or heard of incidences of wife abuse over the years.

These things also occur daily in our community (where we live), in our families, and in case we had simply forgotten.
It was discovered that career and education had an impact on the frequency and type of violence against women as well as whether or not their children saw it.
But we still have some reservations.

These precautions have only slightly contributed to stopping and lessening this repulsive conduct.

This is because the majority of abused women and wives do not express any complaints about being beaten and do not consider the conduct to be wrong. not even on how it impacts a third party that is involved in their life.

This is a result of people's ignorance of the fact that abuse is largely similar to a contagious disease in that it affects and is perpetrated against all members of society, whether directly or indirectly when one person is harmed.

As we all know, children and society are much more deeply connected and significantly impacted by this barbaric act/attitude than women.

Let's look at it from this perspective: it is horrifying to watch a young woman who has a pleasant existence at her place of upbringing "sold" off to another guy just to be abused and molested, but it is incomparable to the case of a child who is born or adopted into this chaos known as life.

This means that a particular generation may have to endure chaos and suffering for the rest of their lives.

The aforementioned claim is supported by the observation that abuse victims never fully or completely restore their sanity; instead, they deal with it for the rest of their lives. They are occasionally weary of the emotions; all they want to see is people experiencing those exact emotions; they never return to how they were before the abuse.

CHAPTER ONE

DEFINITION OF TERMS

- **WIFE BATTERING:-**

Wife battering is referred to as a violent act, such as a psychological, sexual, or physical attack committed by an aggressor against their victim or by a husband against his wife or partner, to restrain the person by causing dread and suffering.

In the absence of the aforementioned, we must have seen it in our neighborhood. Wife battering can also occur with direct victims or the opposite.

Who Are The Factors That Inspire Domestic Violence?

<u>THE ABUSED AND BATTERED WIVES:</u>
The battered wives do not see any need to report to the appropriate authorities due to one reason or the other.

<u>THE ABUSERS:</u>
The abusers derive joy and some manner of satisfaction from this act.

<u>THE SECOND-HAND VICTIMS (THE CHILDREN):</u>
The children of these battered women are also contributors to this societal ill attitude in the sense that they refuse to reach out for necessary help.

NEIGHBORS:

• **DOMESTIC VIOLENCE:-**

Domestic violence disproportionately affects women worldwide, and women typically face more severe types of violence. Additionally, they are more likely than men to defend themselves by using intimate partner violence. Domestic violence may be justifiable or legally allowed in some nations, especially when the woman is involved and there has been actual or alleged adultery. Research has shown that domestic violence rates and gender equality levels are directly and significantly correlated, with domestic violence rates being greater in nations with lower gender equality. For both men and women, domestic abuse is one of the crimes with the lowest global reporting rates. Additionally, because of social stigmas associated with male victimization, victims of domestic violence face an increased likelihood of being overlooked by healthcare providers.

When an abuser thinks they are entitled to it, or that it is appropriate, justifiable, or unlikely to be reported, domestic violence frequently occurs. Children and other family members who believe such abuse is appropriate or encouraged may perpetuate a cycle of violence across generations as a result. Many people mistakenly think of their experiences as out-of-control family conflicts, which prevents them from realizing they are abusers or victims.

Domestic abuse awareness, perception, definition, and documentation vary greatly from nation to nation. Additionally, forced or child marriages frequently result in domestic violence.

In violent relationships, there may be a cycle of abuse where tensions grow, an act of violence is performed, and then there is a period of calm.

The victims may get entrenched in abusive relationships through isolation, dominance, and power, traumatic attachment to the abuser, social acceptance, a lack of resources, fear, humiliation, or the need to protect children. Victims of abuse may have physical impairments, uncontrolled aggression, long-term health issues, mental disease, restricted financial resources, and a limited capacity to form good relationships. Serious mental illnesses like post-traumatic stress disorder might affect victims (PTSD). Children who are raised in violent homes frequently have psychological symptoms of such.

Early-life issues include avoidance, excessive vigilance in the face of danger, and dysregulated aggression may cause vicarious traumatization.

In a speech to the British Parliament in 1973, Jack Ashley used the phrase "domestic violence" for the first time in a modern context to refer to violence that occurs within the house. Before now, the phrase primarily referred to civic disturbance and domestic violence as opposed to external violence.

Domestic violence (DV) has typically been linked primarily to physical abuse. The use of phrases like "wife abuse," "wife beating," "wife battering," and "battered woman" has decreased as efforts have been made to include unmarried couples, non-physical violence, female abusers, and same-sex partnerships. DV is currently widely used as a broad definition that encompasses "any acts of physical, sexual, psychological, or economic violence" that may be committed by a relative or close companion.

The terms domestic violence and intimate partner violence are frequently used interchangeably.

The UN Declaration on the Elimination of Violence Against Women defined domestic violence as:

- Physical, Sexual, and Psychological violence occurring in the family (including battering, sexual abuse of female children in the household, dowry-related violence, marital rape, female genital mutilation and other traditional practices harmful to women, non-spousal violence, and violence related to exploitation.

In a speech to the British Parliament in 1973, Jack Ashley used the phrase "domestic violence" for the first time in a modern context to refer to violence that occurs within the house. Before now, the phrase primarily referred to civic disturbance and domestic violence as opposed to external violence.

Domestic violence (DV) has typically been linked primarily to physical abuse. The use of phrases like "wife abuse," "wife beating," "wife battering," and "battered woman" has decreased as efforts have been made to include unmarried couples, non-physical violence, female abusers, and same-sex partnerships. DV is now widely understood to mean "all acts of domestic violence.

CHAPTER TWO

CAUSES AND REASONS FOR WIFE BATTERING; WHY WOULD SOMEONE BEAT THEIR WIFE?

Although one does not have to be married to be a victim of battering, there are millions of cases of wife abuse reported each year in the United States. Battering can also occur in same-sex relationships. Anyone can become a victim of a wife-beating, regardless of color, social level, or educational background. (Wondering whether you've experienced wife abuse. Test your battered woman status.)

Battered spouses frequently come from homes where they are trained to be submissive and not voice their problems, which ultimately leads them into a relationship that is comparable to that of an adult. It is more likely that men who grew up in families where wife abuse took place while they were teenagers will go on to abuse their wives.

Causes Of Wife Battering.

There is no specific cause for the wife's beating because it is an inherent tendency. One cannot beat another because of a wife or any other circumstance. It's critical to comprehend this because, despite what the batterer may claim, victims frequently blame themselves for being abused.

Within a relationship, though, there is typically a pattern of wife battering (read

Cycle of Violence and Abuse). The phases are typical:

1. A tension-building phase.
2. A wife battering episode.
3. A "honeymoon" phase where there is a respite.

The woman frequently "walks on eggshells" around her batterer during the phase of tension-building and is aware that the tension is rising. Small things like an unpleasant meal or his wife's tardiness can enrage the batterer. Unreasonable tension in the relationship is brought on by these tiny offenses.

The result of this strain is a severe bout of wife abuse. The assault could consist of a large blow or a small push or slap.

This tension eventually explodes in an acute wife battering episode. The battering may be a more minor push or slap or maybe a major beating leading to bone breaking or worse from beating. The abuser might stop the victim from getting medical attention.

After the acute battering is finished, the batterer frequently tries to charm his way out of what happened by swearing never to do it again and making amends by purchasing flowers and being more watchful. However, in most cases, the wife batterer has no intention of stopping and is merely attempting to persuade the victim that she shouldn't tell anybody because "it's not that awful" and "it's all in her brain." The reasons why husbands beat their spouses are further complicated by other societal expectations.

• They believe it's the only way to show their strength.

• They have the impression that the women are more behaved and submissive to them if disciplined physically.

• Most unenlightened youths believe that an undisciplined young girl grows to be a disobedient wife to her husband.

CHAPTER THREE

WHY DO BATTERED WIVES STAY?

A battered wife may prefer to stay in uncommon relationships for a diversity of purposes.

- Battered wives continually think the abuse isn't "real," or "isn't that bad"; they most likely think they can change the abuser.

Nevertheless, they completely forgot; "You cannot change someone else; only they can decide to change themselves."

- They believe it when they are told that "it will never happen again."

- They think help won't work or that no one will believe them or maybe they deserve the abuse.

When they are held accountable for the problems in their relationship, this occurs.

In any situation involving wife-battery, it's critical to avoid placing blame or passing judgment because victims frequently feel terrible already, and further guilt could lead them to think that they deserve the abuse. They might be even more hesitant to quit their batterers as a result of this.

- They don't want to be held responsible for a broken home or family.

- She stays with the batterer because she feels sorry for him as he came from a history containing abuse.

- She chooses to stay because she is either economically or psychologically dependent on the batterer.

- They feel the situation hasn't gotten so dirty that they should leave; maybe because they are only beaten once in a while.

My beloved, "Simply because he only hit you once, that doesn't make it okay. Once is one too many times."

- She is afraid to leave.

- Because of the fears for the welfare of others (like their children).

There are several reasons why a battered wife could continue to be in a relationship. Battered wives often:

They are reliant on the battery both financially and psychologically.
To leave makes them nervous.
They fear for other people's safety (like their children).

Of course, any amount of wife abuse is unacceptable, and any victimized wives should get help right away.

1. <u>Distorted Thoughts.</u>

Being traumatized by control and injury can result in bewilderment, uncertainty, and even self-blame. Victims are harassed and falsely accused by the perpetrators, which wears them down and fills them with guilt. 3 Women expressed things like, "I thought I deserved it," "I was ashamed, embarrassed, and blamed myself because I thought I triggered him," and other similar things. As a coping mechanism, some people downplayed the abuse, saying: "[I stayed] because I didn't think that emotional and financial abuse was abuse. I didn't realize what my boyfriend did to me was rape because "words don't leave bruises" and "Because words don't create marks."

2. <u>Damaged Self-Worth.</u>

Related to this was the harm that such demeaning treatment causes to one's self. He made me feel like I was alone and useless, many women said, adding that they felt as though they had done something wrong and deserved it.

3. <u>Fear.</u>

Abusers employ the potent deterrent of physical and emotional suffering to subdue and trap their victims. 4 Male victims of violence are far less likely to experience dread and distress than female victims. 5 One person commented, "I was scared of him... I anticipated that he would make leaving a painful ordeal. It is risky to attempt to escape an abuser. Due to her husband's "threats of tracking me down, murdering all my loved ones including our kids while I watched, and ultimately killing me," one woman felt imprisoned.

4. <u>Wanting to be a Savior.</u>

Many spoke of wanting to transform their spouses through love or support: "I thought I could love the abuse out of him." Some tweets, such as "I believed I would be the strong one who would never leave him and show him loyalty," highlighted internal values or commitments to the marriage or partner. I would repair him and instill love in him. Others were sympathetic and prioritized their partner's needs over their own: "His father passed away, he developed an alcohol problem, and he said God wouldn't want me to leave him because he wanted me to make him better."

5. <u>Children.</u>

In addition, some mothers prioritized their children over their safety: "I was frightened that if he wasn't abusing me, he would abuse his kids. And I placed more value on their lives than on me. Additionally, "I stayed for 20 years, protecting our children all the while I was being abused." Some people said they stayed for the benefit of the kids: "I wanted my son to have a father."

6. <u>Family Expectations and Experiences.</u>

Many people shared accounts of how prior encounters with violence damaged their sense of self or their ability to form good relationships: "I observed [my dad] hitting my mother. Then I met someone who reminded me of my father, "You partner with wolves since you were nurtured among animals." Some people spoke of pressures from their families and religion: "My mother told me God would disown me if I destroyed my marriage."

7. <u>Financial Constraints.</u>

Numerous others mentioned their financial struggles, which were frequently related to taking care of Chattering because he was alone with two young children, had no family and was also feeling guilty due to brain damage from a car accident. Others were financially exploited by their abuser: "[My] ex built up thousands of debt in my name." Others were unable to maintain employment due to the abuser's control or their disabilities.

8. <u>Isolation.</u>

Separating their victims from family and friends is a frequent method used by manipulative spouses. As one lady discovered: "I was imprisoned in the backwoods of WV, and he would exploit my tiny boy to keep me close," this can occasionally take the form of physical abuse. As one woman was told: "You can either have friends and family or you can have me," isolation can also be emotionally draining at times.

It may be difficult for a battered wife to recognize unhealthy relationships because she grew up in a family where abuse was accepted. This is another reason why she decides to stay. He seems to adore her, therefore she might decide to stay to be sorry for the brutality She could wish to make an effort to maintain the connection while assisting his growth. Due to her self-blame, she might continue.

CHAPTER FOUR

HANDLING ISSUES OF WIFE BATTERING

While we work to find a long-term solution to the problem of wife-battering in marriages and our cultures, it's equally important to take into account the issue that wives themselves must address. That is the problem with the running mouth.

This is not my attempt to excuse wife abuse, but to reduce the problem of wife abuse, wives must learn that the power of the tongue should not be used negatively to resolve conflicts in marriage. Every woman must understand that, despite being little, the mouth and tongue are extremely powerful and, as such, can end the planet.

The power of the mouth is best summed up by the proverb "It is with the mouth that the world was formed, and the mouth that it will be destroyed."; "It won't die from my mouth."

Many relationships have failed as a result of bad-mouthing one another. It is a known fact that many marital disputes that end in wife abuse begin with verbal abuse by the husbands. During arguments, a wife may speak negatively about her husband in such a way that the husband may become irrational and behave badly. Typically, the outcome is unpleasant.

My modest view and counsel to the women is that even the smallest of things can enrage the batterer, such as when his wife is late for dinner or when he uses harsh or nasty language against them. Unreasonable tension in the relationship is brought on by these tiny offenses.

An intense session of wife abuse eventually causes the strain to burst. The beating could be a light push or slap or it could be a serious beating that results in fractured bones or even worse.

In extreme situations, the abuser could stop the victim from seeking medical attention for their wounds and intimidate them into keeping the abuse to themselves or others.

which even worsens the act according to
how it is seen.

After the acute battering is finished, we
frequently observe that the batterer tries to
charm his way out of what has happened by
swearing never to do it again and making
amends by purchasing flowers, gifts, and
being extra attentive.
The wife batterer typically has no intention
of stopping, but instead is just trying to trick
the victim into keeping it a secret by
convincing her that "it's not that horrible"
and that it's "all in her brain."

Her worry that she might not be receiving
the assistance and care she needs to resist
the unfair act against her may sometimes be
the root of this notion.

Or if she thinks it's acceptable for a man to hit his wife periodically.

Not! The time has come for our women to realize that no level of wife abuse, no matter how infrequent, is acceptable. Additionally, any wife who has been a victim of abuse should seek help right away.

CHAPTER FIVE

HOW DO YOU EXPOSE AN ABUSER?

Here's how to expose an abuser without any fear of getting hurt:

1. Write your story.
2. First, you should understand that your silence will encourage your abuser to abuse you or someone else again.
3. Express everything you've been through.
4. Choose the right platform.
5. Let people know.

CHAPTER SIX

PERSUADING A BATTERED WIFE TO LEAVE.

Is it even right and acceptable to advise a beaten wife to end her marriage or leave her home?

It is frequently necessary to persuade a battered wife to quit her batterer by dispelling her erroneous perceptions of the abuse.

An abused wife frequently needs a place to stay, such as a friend's home or a shelter for battered women. A woman may be influenced to leave her batterer if she considers the needs and safety of the wife,

any children, and occasionally the pets
(which may also be mistreated).

In any situation involving wife abuse, it's
critical to avoid placing blame and passing
judgment because the victims frequently feel
terrible already, and further guilt could lead
them to believe that they are to blame for the
abuse. They could become even more
hesitant to leave their abused wife as a result
of this.

CHAPTER SEVEN

SOME FACTS ABOUT WIFE BATTERING

The Facts About Wife Battering.

In the United States, the CDC estimates that more than 1 in 3 women and almost 1 in 3 males will suffer intimate partner violence in their lifetime. Teens who date violently makeup one in three. People who identify as nonbinary or LGBTQ+ are frequently at an even higher risk of being abused.

Compared to white women, black women are 35% more likely to experience domestic abuse.

Although domestic violence affects people of all income levels, it affects lower-income households more frequently than higher-income households. 7 times as many women with household incomes of less than $7,500 as men.
 Equally as likely to encounter domestic violence as women whose households make over $75,000. (Source)

Abuse, which is exacerbated by homophobia and transphobia, is frequently even more likely to occur to those who identify as nonbinary or LGBTQ+. Compared to survivors who did not identify as transgender women, transgender women who experienced intimate partner violence (IPV) were about 2.5 times more likely to face sexual assault and nearly 4 times more likely to experience financial abuse. (Source)

According to national statistics, at least 45% of victims of domestic abuse say their abuser sexually attacked them.

CHAPTER EIGHT

IMPACT AND EFFECTS OF DOMESTIC VIOLENCE ON CHILDREN

IMPACT

Children that reside in abusive homes are always impacted by it. According to research, the most significant risk factor for child maltreatment may be abuse in the family. Children can be harmed by abuse even if they are not aware of it. Children who are abused go through a lot of pain, but children who witness abuse also experience pain. Children witness the effects of the abuse after it has already happened. Injuries including bruises ripped clothing, broken

items, splintered furniture, holes in the
walls, swollen faces, and puffy eyes could
be visible. They sense the abuser's tension
and fear and don't feel safe.

Every year, 1 in 15 children are exposed to
intimate partner violence, and 90% of these
kids have seen the violence firsthand.
(NCADV)

Children are especially susceptible to being
victims of, or witnesses to, assault, sexual
abuse, and domestic violence. We must step
in and offer services if we want to stop the
cycle of violence. (NNEDV)

In homes with a high prevalence of domestic
violence, the rate of child abuse or grave

neglect is 1,500% higher than the national norm.

Children affected by domestic violence are more likely to be neglected, and more than half of them experience physical abuse.

Children's physical, cognitive, psychological, and social development can be severely hampered by directly or indirectly witnessing abuse. Children frequently get caught in conflict, too. Teenagers usually think that they are to blame for the abuse, that if they were better, it would not have happened, or that they could have stopped it if they were good enough.

EFFECTS

Physical Abuse And Neglect:

In addition to a higher chance of child abuse and neglect, kids run the risk of getting wounded while defending their moms or getting caught in the crossfire.

Physical Ailments:

Children may experience physical problems like headaches, rashes, ulcers, and autoimmune disorders as a result of stress.

Aggression And Difficulty Interacting With Peers:

Some kids imitate the hostility and violence they have witnessed at home. As a way of protecting themselves, other kids could isolate themselves socially.

Common Behaviors:

Children may experience loss of appetite, night terrors, nervousness around strangers, tantrums, and bedwetting. These kids frequently experience speech or hearing issues as well as learning impairments.

CHAPTER NINE

COMMON CHARACTERISTICS OF CHILDREN FROM VIOLENT FAMILIES

Children from violent households are more likely to exhibit the following traits and behaviors. Naturally, not all of these youngsters exhibit these traits, and many manage to flee from abuse with relatively intact personalities. Additionally, many of these traits may be present in kids from households without physical abuse. However, some patterns overwhelmingly point to experiencing or seeing violence.

1. Withdrawn/apathetic behavior, childhood depression, unsocial,

passive, feelings of powerlessness, moody, overly controlled, poor self-concept.

2. Aggressive/violent behavior: anger, open rage, low frustration tolerance, poorly socialized, difficult to control, low self-esteem.

3. Shame and humiliation in belonging to a deviant family.

4. Feelings of guilt and responsibility for family violence.

5. Stigma: feelings of being different.

6. Physical fears.

7. Fear of intimacy: distrustful, armored, vigilant.

8. Distrustful of males (males and females).

9. Identification with the aggressor (mostly males).

10. Identification with victims (mostly females).

11. Confused values: physical force is viewed as a legitimate means of control (particularly control of women by men); "Might is right." "Nice guys finish last."

12. Conflicting and ambivalent feelings and loyalties toward parents: feelings of love/hate for both parents; anger, pity, and contempt for the person abused; anger, fear, and respect for an abusive person.

13. Parental child: precocious mothering, role reversal.

14. Physical problems and complaints.

15. Learning problems.

16. Sexual behavior is seen as an expression of power and anger rather than of love and tenderness.

TYPES OF ABUSE.

The majority of States identify physical abuse, neglect, sexual abuse, and emotional abuse as the four main categories of maltreatment. A lot of States also classify parental drug usage, human trafficking, and desertion as forms of abuse or neglect.

CONSEQUENCES OF DOMESTIC VIOLENCE.

Consequences include a rise in the prevalence of posttraumatic stress disorder, depression, anxiety, and suicide as well as an increased risk of cardiovascular disease and early mortality. Violence has different health effects depending on the victim's age, gender, and the type of violence used.

CHAPTER TEN

THE DANGERS OF DOMESTIC VIOLENCE AND THE IMPORTANCE OF PREVENTION

Any sort of abuse or violence has detrimental effects on the victim's health. Chronic pain, an elevated risk of stroke, heart disease, lung illness, diabetes, cancer, or gynecological issues are just a few of the detrimental health effects it can cause. Additionally, there are behavioral health issues such as high-risk sexual habits, alcoholism, and depression. Domestic violence is also associated with absenteeism and subpar performance at work, which can lead to social isolation, housing problems, financial difficulties, and additional health risks for victims and their families.

How You Can Help Victims of Domestic Violence

If you know someone in an abusive relationship, there are ways you can help.

<u>Listen:</u> If at all feasible, arrange a private, secure time and location where you can speak with your friend or relative. Begin the dialogue by expressing worry, such as with "I'm concerned for your safety." Give your friend or family member the floor and express your belief in what they have to say.

<u>Offer Support:</u> Make sure they understand they are not alone and that no one should suffer harm. The victim of abuse is not at fault. Tell them that what they are feeling is acceptable. Next, find out how you can help them the most.

Provide Resources: Encourage them to contact neighborhood resources. Provide them with any further resources they may require, such as crisis hotlines, support groups, domestic violence shelters, mental health services, etc.

Help Safety Plan: Make a safety plan with your family or friends.

Respect Their Choices: Do not compel them to leave. Never is it as easy as merely leaving. People continue to be in abusive relationships for a variety of reasons. Provide them with resources and assistance, but understand that in the end, it is their choice. Keep your opinions to yourself and don't make them feel bad for continuing an abusive relationship. Tell them you'll support them no matter what decision they make.

Keep in mind that your role is to help your loved one, not to save or rescue them.

CONCLUSION

One of the most horrifying forms of abuse that women experience in our culture today is domestic violence. According to statistics, 85 percent of victims of domestic violence are women. Men make up only 15% of victims. No matter the victim's color, faith, religion, or social status, domestic violence can affect anyone.

Domestic abuse will persist indefinitely among all social classes if the problem is not addressed adequately. For our society to prevent this dreadful form of abuse, we must band together and enact stricter legislation that will safeguard the abuse victims.